THE WORLD'S MISTAKE
IN
OLIVER CROMWELL

by

SLINGSBY BETHEL

Published by *The Rota* at the University of Exeter
1972

Printed in Great Britain by
Scolar Press Limited, Menston, Yorkshire

Slingsby Bethel (1617–97), a principal exponent of the notion of 'interest' after the Restoration, here argues that England's interest lies in increasing trade and keeping the balance among her neighbours. It was therefore ill-served by Oliver's foreign policy which put his private interest above that of the nation. Closely examining the situation and the protectorate's foreign policy, Bethel asserts that Cromwell mistakenly went to war against Spain, thus strengthening France, when *raison d'état* dictated peace. Cromwell's Baltic policy was equally foolish; even had it succeeded it would have broken the balance of power there. Thus, the world has been wrong to regard Oliver as an able statesman; and furthermore, in internal affairs, he frequently acted unjustly and tyrannically.

On Cromwell's foreign policy, see Christopher Hill, *God's Englishman* (London, 1971), esp. Chap. 6; Michael Roberts, 'Cromwell and the Baltic', *Essays in Swedish History* (London, 1967); and Roger Crabtree, 'The idea of a Protestant foreign policy', *The Cromwell Association Handbook*, 1968/69 (London, 1969). For a discussion of 'interest', see J. A. W. Gunn, *Politics and the public interest in the seventeenth century* (London and Toronto, 1969).

Examination of the copies of *The world's mistake* in the British Museum (4), the Bodleian Library (3), Columbia University and Goldsmiths' Library, University of London (3) revealed that there were three variant printings of the edition of 1668. The fullest of these (Eagle 1) consists of ii plus 21 pp; its title page bears a double-headed eagle. Each of the other two variants omits part of the text but they were produced not only from the same type, but in so far as possible, by keeping the same lines, the deletions being made up by moving the type, thus changing the pages which were also respaced. The second variant (Eagle 2) also bears the eagle on its title page but its pages are misnumbered. The third variant (Ornaments) has a new title page on which the eagle has been replaced by rows of ornaments; the pages are correctly numbered and their spacing has been improved. The passages deleted from the variant reproduced here are as follows: thirty-seven lines from 'And were' p. 10, l. 11) to 'against Spain' (p. 11, l. 10); forty-one lines from 'Holland could not' (p. 18, l. 16) to 'peopled in Italy' (p. 19, l. 17); and four lines from 'so that' (p. 19, l. 22) to 'Publick good'. The fullest version seems to be the earliest; the text makes better sense with the passages in rather than out, for example, the conclusion (p. 19) that countries prosper, regardless of whether they are

Catholic or Protestant, if church lands are alienated and toleration prevails, is established by the numerous instances omitted from the shorter variants.

The world's mistake has been reproduced from a copy in the Goldsmiths' Library, University of London Library, with the permission of the Director.

Wing, *Short title catalogue*, B2079, records only one version.

THE ǁ.
WORLD·S MISTAKE
IN
Oliver Cromwell;
OR,
A short Political Discourse,
SHEWING,

That CROMWELL'S Mal-admi-
niftration, (during his *Four Years*, and
Nine Moneths pretended Protectorfhip,)
layed the Foundation of our prefent Condition, in the Decay of TRADE.

LONDON,
Printed in the Year MDCLXVIII.

The *World's Mistake* in *Oliver Cromwell*, &c.

O F all the Sins, that the Children of Men are guilty of, there is none, that our corrupt Natures are more inclinable unto, than that of *Idolatry*, a Sin, that may be towards Men, so well as other Creatures, and things; For, as that which a Man unmeasurably relyes, and setts his Heart upon, is Called his G O D, even as that which he falls down before, and worshippeth : so, when one hath the Person of another in an excess of admiration, whether for Greatness or Richness, &c. which we are subject to adore, we are said to Idolize him; and therefore the wise *Venetians*, who, of all men, are most Jealous of their Liberty, Considering that as the nature of Man is not prone to any thing more than the Adoration of Men, So nothing is more destructive to Freedom, hath, for preventing the Mischiefs of it, made it unlawfull, even so much as to mourn for their Duke at his death; Intimating thereby, that their Felicity and Safety depends not upon the uncertain Thred of any one Man's life; but upon the Vertue of their good Laws, and Orders, well executed, and that they can never want vertuous Persons to succeed : and how do such Principles in men, lead by little more than Moralitie, reprove those, who have a great measure of Gospel-light, for their senseless excess, in their adoring the remembrance of *Cromwell*. For as the Objects of Idolatry are mistaken Creatures, or things, proceeding some times from self-love, so well as other Causes, So the undeserved approbation, and applause, that *Cromwell*'s memory seems to have with his Adherents, amounting to little less, than the Idolizing of him, appears to me, to be the product of an excessive Veneration of Greatness, and a selfish Partiality towards him; for that the more honour is given to him, the more prayse they think will consequently redound to

them,

them, who were his Favourites; and they fortifie themfelves herein, with the Credit they fay he hath abroad, though there is little in that, becaufe the opinion that Strangers have of him, may well be put upon the accompt of their ignorance, in the Affairs of *England*, which Travellers do finde, to be fo great, even amongft Minifters of State, as is to be admired. And now as this Error in Idolizing *Oliver* hath two moral Evils in it, (befides the fin in it felf:) The one, a reflection upon the prefent times, as if the former were better than thefe; And the other, the unjuft defrauding the *Long Parliament* of that which is due to them, to give it Idolitroufly to him, to whom it doth not belong; I efteem it a Duty incumbent upon me, to difcover the Miftake. I am not infenfible, that I fhall by this, draw the envye of thofe upon me, who, being Jealous of their Honour, will be angry for touching them in their *Diana*; but knowing my felf clear, from the Vices of envying Vertue in any, how contrary foever he may be to me in Judgment, fo well, as from being unwilling to allow every one their due Commendations, I will caft my felf upon Providence, for the fuccefs of this Paper; And in reference to *Cromwell*s Government, and the prefent times, make fome Obfervations relating to both, and, in order thereunto, fhew,

Firft, That the original caufe of the low condition that we are now (in relation to Trade) reduced unto, had it's beginning in *Olivers* time, and the foundations of it, layed, either, by his ignorant miftaking the Intereft of this Kingdome, or wilfully doing it, for the advancement of his own particular Intereft.

Secondly, That his time, for the fhort continuance, had as much of oppreffion, and injuftice, as any former times.

Thirdly and laftly, That he never in his later dayes, valued either honour or honefty, when they ftood in the way of his ambition, and that there is nothing to be admired in him (though fo much Idolized) but that the partiallity of the world, fhould make him fo great a favorite of ignorance, and forgetfullnefs, as he feems to be.

When this late Tyrant, or Protector, (as fome calls him) turned out the Long Parliament, the Kingdome was arrived at the
higheft

highest pitch of Trade, Wealth, and Honour, that it, in any Age, ever yet knew. The Trade appeared, by the great Sums offered then for the Customes and Excise, Nine hundred thousand pounds a year, being refused. The Riches of the Nation, shewed it self, in the high value, that Land, and all our Native Commodities bore, which are the certain marks of opulencie. Our Honour, was made known to all the world, by a Conquering Navie, which had brought the proud *Hollanders* upon their Knees, to begg peace of us, upon our own Conditions, keeping all other Nations in awe. And besides these advantages, the publick stock, was Five hundred thousand pounds in ready Money, the value of seven hundred thousand pounds in Stores, and the whole Army in Advance, some four, and none under two months; so that though there might be a debt of near Five hundred thousand pounds upon the Kingdom, he met with above twice the value in lieu of it.

The Nation being in this flourishing and formidable posture, *Cromwell* began his Usurpation, upon the greatest advantages imaginable, having it in his power to have made peace, and profitable Leagues, in what manner he had pleased withall our Neighbours, every one courting us then, and being ambitious of the friendship of *England*; But as if the Lord had infatuated, and deprived him of common sence and reason, he neglected all our golden opportunities, misimproved the Victory God had given us over the *United Netherlands*, making peace (without ever striking stroak) so soon as ever things came into his hands, upon equal tearms with them. And immediately after, contrary to our Interest, made an unjust Warr with *Spain*, and an impollitick League with *France*, bringing the first thereby under, and making the latter too great for Christendome; and by that means, broke the ballance betwixt the two Crowns of *Spain*, and *France*, which his Predecessors the Long Parliament, had alwayes wisely preserved.

In this dishonest Warr with *Spain*, he pretended, and indeavoured, to impose a belief upon the world, that he had nothing in his eye, but the advancement of the Protestant Cause, and the honour of this Nation; but his pretences, were either fraudu-

lent,

lent, or he was ignorant in Forreign affairs (as I am apt to think, that he was not guilty of too much knowledge in them) For he that had known any thing of the temper of the Popish Prelacie, and the French Court pollicies, could not but see, that the way to increafe, or preferve the reformed Intereft in *France*, was by rendring the Proteftants of neceffary ufe to their King, for that longer than they were fo, they could not be free from perfecuti-on, and that the way to render them fo, was by keeping the bal-lance betwixt *Spain* and *France* even, as that, which would con-fequently make them ufefull to their King: But by overthrow-ing the ballance in his Warr with *Spain*, and joyning with *France*, he freed the French King from his fears of *Spain*, inabled him to fubdue all Factions at home, and thereby to bring himfelf into a condition of not ftanding in need of any of them, and from thence, hath proceeded the perfecution that hath fince been, and ftill is, in that Nation, againft the reformed there; fo that *Oliver*, inftead of advancing the reformed Intereft, hath by an error in his Polliticks, been the Author of deftroying it.

The Honour and Advantage, he propounded to this Nation, in his pulling down of *Spain*, had as ill a foundation : For if true, as was faid, that we were to have had *Oftend*, and *Newport*, fo well as *Dunkirk* (when we could get them) they bore no proportion in any kind, to all the reft of the King of *Spains* European Domi-nions, which muft neceffarily have fallen to the French Kings fhare, becaufe of their joyning, and nearnefs to him, and remote-nefs from us, and the increafing the greatnefs of fo near a Neigh-bour, muft have increafed our future dangers: But this man, who through ignorance, is fo ftrangely cryed up in the world, was not guilty of this error in State only, but committed as great a folecifme, in his defigning the outing of the King of *Denmark*, and fetting up of the King of *Sweden* : For had the *Sweeds*, but got *Copenhagen*, (as in all probability had *Oliver* lived, they would have done) they had wanted nothing of confequence, but the Cities of *Lubeck* and *Dantzigge*, (which by their then potencie, they would eafily have gained) of being Mafters of the whole *Baltick* Sea, on both fides, from the Sound or mouth down to the bottome of it; by which, together with all *Denmark*, *Norway*, and

and the *Danes*, part of *Holstein*, which would consequently have been theirs (they then having as they still have the Land of *Bremen*) there would have been nothing, but the small Counties of *Ouldenburge*, and *East-Friezland*, (which would easily have fallen into their mouths) betwixt them, and the *United Netherlands*, whereby *Sweden*, would on the one side to the North, and North-East, have been as great, as *France* on the other, to the South, and South-West; and they two, able to have divided the Western Empire betwixt them.

And whereas, it had in all Ages been the policies of the Northern States and Potentates, to keep the Dominion of the *Baltick* Sea, devided amongst several pettie Princes and States, that no one might be sole Master of it; becaufe otherwife, moft of the neceffary Commodities for shipping, coming from thence and *Norway*, any one Lord of the whole, might lay up the shipping of *Europe*, by the walls, in shutting only of his Ports, and denying the Commodities of his Country to other States. *Cromwell* contrary to this wife Maxime, endeavoured to put the whole *Baltick* Sea into the *Sweeds* hands, and undoubtedly had (though I suppose ignorantly) done it, if his death had not given them that succeeded him, the Long Parliament, an opportunity of prudently preventing it: For if he had underftood the importance of the *Baltick* Sea to this Nation, he could not have been fo impolitick, as to have projected fo dangerous a defign againft his new *Utopia*, as giving the opening and shutting of it to any one Prince. I am not ignorant, that this error is excufed, by pretending that we were to have had *Elfinore* and *Cronenburge* Castle, (the firft, the Town, upon the narrow entrance of the *Baltick*, called the Sound, where all Ships Rides, and payes Toll to the King of *Denmark*; and the latter, the Fortrefs, that defends both Town and Ships,) by which we fhould have been Mafters of the Sound, and confequently of the *Baltick*; but they that knows thofe Countries, and how great a Prince the *Sweed* would have been, had he obtained all the reft, befides thefe two Bables, muft confefs, we fhould have been at his devotion, in our holding of any thing in his Countries: And further, if the dangerous confequence of fetting up fo great a Prince, had not been in the cafe, it

had

had been againſt the Intereſt of *England* to have had an obligation upon us to maintain places ſo remote, againſt the enmity of many States and Princes; and that for theſe reaſons :

Firſt, becauſe the ordinary Tolls of the Sound, would not have defrayed half the charge, and to have taken more than the ordinary Tolls, we could not have done, without drawing a generall quarrel upon us, from moſt of the Princes, and States of the Northern parts of *Europe*.

Secondly, becauſe the experience of all former times ſheweth us, that foreign acquiſitions, have ever been Chargeable, and prejudicial to the people of *England*, as Sir *Robert Cotton* makes it clearly appear, That not only all thoſe Pieces of *France*, which belonged to us by rightfull ſucceſſion; but alſo thoſe we held by Conqueſt, were alwayes great burthens to our Nation, and cauſe of much poverty and miſery to the People. And it is not our Caſe alone, to be the worſe for Conqueſts, (although more ours, than other Countries, becauſe of the Charge and uncertainty of the Windes and Weather in the Tranſportation of Succours and relief by Sea, which contiguous Territories, which are upon the Maine, are not ſubject to,) but the Caſe alſo of (I think I may ſay) all other Kingdoms. In *France*, their burthens and oppreſſions have grown in all ages, with the greatneſs of their Kings ; Nay, even after their laſt peace with *Spain*, by which they had given them peace with all the world, beſides many places in the *Spaniſh Netherlands*, and *Catalonia* into boot : Upon which the poor people promiſed themſelves (though vainly) an unqueſtionable abatement of Taxes; inſtead of that, they found their preſſures increaſed dayly, and though their King, overgrownly great and rich himſelf, yet the people ſo poor, that thouſands are ſaid to dye in a plentifull year, for want of bread to their water, nothing being free there, but freſh water and aire ; For (except in ſome few priviledged places) wherever they have the conveniencie by their Situation of Sea water, (leaſt they ſhould make uſe of the benefit of that, which God and Nature hath given them, for ſaving the charge of Salt,) every family is forced to take ſo much Salt of the King, at his own rate, (which is above ten times the price it is ſold for to ſtrangers, for

tranſ-

transportation) as is judged they may spend in a year ; the Lord deliver all other Countries from their example. In *Sweden*, that King, Court, and their Military Officers, are the better for their Conquests, in *Germany*, *Denmark*, *Russia*, and some places antiently belonging to *Poland* ; but the Commons the worse : *Spain* is undone, by the great number of people sent thence to the *west-Indies*, which hath depopulated the Country , *France* reaping more benefit by keeping their people at home to Manufactures, than *Spain* doth by sending theirs abroad for Silver and Gold; and now, though by these instances it may appear to be the Interest of the people of other Nations, so well as ours, to live in peace, without coveting additions ; yet it is more our true Interest, (because, by reason of our Situation, we have no need of Forreign Frontier Towns, our Ships well ordered, being better than other Princes bordering Garrisons) than any other Kingdoms to neglect especially *Europian* acquisition, and colonies, and apply our selves :

First, To the improving of our own Land, of which we have more than we have people to manage.

Secondly, To the Increasing our Home and Forreign Trades, for which we have natural advantages above any other Nation.

Thirdly and Lastly, to make use of our strength (which Trade will increase) together with the helps that God and Nature hath given us in our Situation, and otherwise, to the keeping the Ballance amongst our Neighbours ; For if the Province of *Holland*, which is but Four hundred thousand Acres of profitable ground, is by the benefit of Trade able to do so much, as we experienced the last Warr, what might we do, if Trade were improved, who have much more advantages for it, than they have : I ascribe what was done by the *Netherlands* in the late Warr to the Province of *Holland* ; because, that though the Provinces are seven in number, *Hollands* due proportion of all charges, is $58\frac{1}{3}$ in a hundred, to all the others $41\frac{2}{3}$, of which $41\frac{2}{3}$, *Holland* gets little more than 20. honestly paid them, insomuch, that it alone may be reckoned to bear four fifths in a hundred, to one fifth that all the other six bears ; and how prodigious a thing is it, that *Holland*, no bigger than as before mentioned, should be able to

B Coap

Coap with *England*, *Scotland*, and *Ireland* ; and that though their Charges in the late Warr was abundantly greater than ours, yet by their good management, to be fo little the worfe for it, that at the conclufion of the Warr, to have their Credits fo high, that they could have commanded what Money they had pleafed at Three in the Hundred, and all this by the meer additional benefit of Trade and good Order ; and how by *Cromwells* indifcreet neg-lecting of Trade, and choofing Warr when he was in Peace did he mifs the true Intereft of *England*, as by his ill founded de-figns, he did the Intereft of the Reformed Religion ; For if he had fucceeded in his unjuft Invafion of the Spanifh Territories in the *weft-Indies*, (as God feldome profpereth difhoneft under-takings) it being intended for a State acquifition, the benefit would not have been defufive, but chiefly to himfelf and Favo-rites, and prejudicial to the people in generall, though at the ex-pence of their fubftance, the acquefts would have been made : For had he met with fo much fuccefs in the gaining thofe Coun-tries, and in them, that plenty of Gold and Silver as he vain-ly hoped for, we fhould have been as unhappy in them (in the depopulating of our Countries, by the lofs of the multitude of people that muft have been fent thither, and in impoverifhing our Nations by the vaft charge of a continual Warr) as *Spain* is, and to no other end, than the making of him only Rich, able to In-flave the remaining people, and to make himfelf abfolute over them ; for the preventing of which, in fuch Tyrants as *Cromwell*, furely *Mofes* had an eye, when he faid that they fhould not greatly multiply Silver and Gold. And thus, as *Cromwells* defigns muft, to an impartial Judgement, appear to have been laid, fome difho-neftly, others impolitickly, and all contrary to the Intereft of the Kingdome, fo the Iffue of them was dammageable to the people of *England* : As,

Firft, in his fudden making a Peace with *Holland*, fo foon as he got the Government, without thofe advantages for Trade, as they who beat them did intend to have had, as their due, and juft fatisfaction for their Charges in the War.

Secondly, in his War with *Spain*, by the loffe of that benefi-cial Trade to our Nation, and giving it to the *Hollanders*, by

whofe

whofe hands we drave (during the War) the greateft part of that Trade which we had of it, with 25. in the hundreth profit to them, and as much loffe to us.

Thirdly, by our loffe in that War with *Spain*, of 1500 *Englifh* fhips, according as was reported to that Affembly, called *Richards Parliament*.

Fourthly, in the difgracefulleft defeat at *Hifpaniola* that ever this Kingdom fuffered in any age or time.

Fifthly, and laftly, in fpending the great Publick ftock he ound, and yet leaving a vaft Debt upon the Kingdom, as appeared by the Accompts brought into *Richards Affembly*; which had, (I believe) been yet much higher, but that they who under him managed the Affairs, were a fort of People who had been long difciplin'd, (before his time) to a Principle of Frugality, and againft Cheating; though at coufening the poorer People, for their Mafters benefit, fome of them were grown as dexterous, as if they had been bred in the Court of *Spain*; For befides impofing *Richard* upon the People, after his Fathers death, by a forged Title, according to the very Law they took to be in being, when by his Affembly, they were ordered to bring in an Accompt of the Receipts, and payments of the Kingdom; they made about Sixty thoufand pounds fpent in Intelligence, whereas it coft not above Three or Four thoufand at moft; and calculating the reft by thefe, it may well be concluded, that they were expert in their Trades.

It is confeffed, that *Olivers* Peace and League with *France*, was upon honourable Articles; but as the tottering Affaires of *France* then ftood, much more could not have been fooner asked, than had; For *Mazerine*, being a Man of a large and fubtle wit, apprehending the Greatnefs of *England* at that time, which was then dreadfull to the World, and the Vaft advantages *France* would have in pulling down, by their help, of *Spain*, granted him, not onely any thing for the prefent that he demanded, but difregarded alfo, even his Parties making their boafts of the awe he had him under, Confidering, that when *Cromwell* had helped him, to do his Work, in bringing under the Houfe of *Auftria*, and therein cafting the ballance of Chriftendom on his

fide

fide, he fhould afterwards have leifure to recover what then he feemed to part with; And though nothing is more ordinary, than to hear Men bragg, how *Oliver* Vapoured over *France*, I do efteem *Mazerine*'s complying with him, for his own ends, to be the Chief piece of all his Miniftry; For by that means only, and no other, is his Mafter become fo great at this day, that no Factions at home can difturb his Peace, nor Powers abroad frighten him, Which is more than any King of *France*, fince *Charles* the Great, could fay; And when his Neighbour Nations have (too late I fear) experienced his Greatnefs, they will finde caufe to Curfe the ignorance of *Oliver*'s Politicks. And were not this a matter of Fact, frefh in the memory of every one, it were hardly to be believed, that a Man, having had fo large experience of the abilities of his Mafters, the Long Parliament, fhould fo foon as things came into his hands, walk fo contrary to their example, and the true Intereft of *England*, as it appears he did; but by it he fhewed no lefs than his Ignorance in Foreign Affaires, and the true Intereft of Nations; And that he fell into this Error by not underftanding that our Intereft was changed from what it had been about fifteen years before, when it had for eighty years together, at leaft, been our Intereft to fide with *France* againft *Spain*, the Houfe of *Auftria* then being in a fair way (as they had long defigned) of carrying the Univerfal Monarchy; But after *France* in *Anno* 1635. had joyned with *Sweeden* and *Holland*, againft *Spain* and Houfe of *Auftria*, That in *Anno* 1639. the *Spaniard* had loft all their Naval ftrength before *Dover*, being beaten there by the *Dutch*, That in *Anno* 1640. *Portugal*, with all their Eaft and Weft India Plantations, were revolted, That in *Anno* 1641. *Cattalonia* was fallen unto the *French*, the lownefs of the Houfe of *Auftria* then changed our Intereft, and made it to be that of Arbitrators, in keeping the Ballance even, betwixt the two Parties of *Spain* and *France*, which the Long Parliament firft difcovered, and wifely purfued, to the giving a good example to the *Hollanders*, who, fo foon as they had an opportunity, followed it; For at the Treaty at *Munfter*, the *French* (about *anno* 1648.) in a kinde of bravado, giving the *Hollanders*, who were then in League with them, leave

leave to make their Peace with *Spain*, (thinking it was not in their power to do it,) they took the *French* at their words, and immediately ftruck up a Peace with *Spain*; at which the *French* were afterwards fo intenfed, that it is well if they have yet forgot it. But by this means, and the Long Parliaments Neutrality, with a bending towards *Spain*, the Ballance betwixt the two Crownes of *France* and *Spain* was preferved, untill *Cromwell* imprudently broke it, Not knowing (I fuppofe) that Our Intereft was Changed, but thinking it was ftill the fame, and as popular as it had formerly been, to be againft *Spain*; and therefore, when a true meafure is taken of *Cromwell*, the approbation that he hath in the World, will not be found to have its Foundation in fence or reafon, but proceeding from Ignorance, and Atheifme : From Ignorance, in thofe that takes all that was done by him, as a Servant, and whileft under the direction of better Heads, than his own, to be done by him alone ; And from Atheifme, in thofe that thinks every thing lawfull that a man doeth, if it fucceed to his advancement ; But they that fhall take an impartial View of his Actions whileft he was a Single Perfon, and at liberty to make ufe of his own Parts without controll, will finde nothing worthy Commendations, but caufe enough from thence to obferve, that the wifedom of his Mafters, and not his own, muft have been that by which he firft moved; and to attribute his former performances, whileft a Servant, (as is truly due) to the Judgement and Subtilty of the Long Parliament, under whofe Conduct and Command he was. And now from *Cromwells* neglecting to live in peace, as if he had pleafed he might have done with all the World, to the great enriching of this Nation; The improvement of our Victory over *Holland* in his peace with them, His being the Caufe of the loffe of our Spanifh Trade, during all his time, Of the loffe of 1500 Englifh fhips in that War, befides, by it, breaking the Ballance of *Europe*, Of the expence of the Publick Stock and Stores he found, with the contracting a Debt of Nineteen hundred thoufand pounds, according to his own accompt, (which, for ought I know he left behinde him, but am apt to think the Debt was not altogether fo great, though made fo to his Sonne *Richard*'s Affembly, as a

means

means to get the more Money from the poorer people :) And
laftly, of the diſhonourable overthrow we met with at *Hiſpaniola,* It
may well be Concluded that he lay the Foundation of our preſent
want of Trade, to what we formerly enjoyed; and that the reaſon
why his miſcarriages were not ſooner under obſervation, is, becauſe our Stock of Wealth and Honour at his Coming to the
Government, being then unſpeakably great, ſtifled their ap-
pearance, untill having ſince had ſome unhappy additional
Loſſes, they are now become diſcernable as firſt Loſſes to a Mer-
chant, who Concealedly bears up under them, are afterwards
diſcovered by the addition of ſecond Loſſes, that ſincks him :
When I contemplate theſe great Failings, I cannot but appre-
hend the ſadd Condition any people are in, whoſe Governour
drive on a diſtinct contrary Intereſt to theirs; for doubtleſs *Cromwell's* over-weening Care to ſecure his particular Intereſt, againſt
His Majeſty, (then abroad) and the Long Parliament, whom
he had turned out, with a prodigious Ambition of acquiring a
glorious Name in the World, carried him on to all his Miſtakes
and Abſurdities, to the irreparable loſſe and dammage of this famous Kingdom.

To prove the ſecond Aſſertion, That *Oliver's* Time was full
of Oppreſſion and Injuſtice, I ſhall but inſtance in a few of many
Particulars, and begin with *John Lilburne,* not that I think him
in any kinde one that deſerved favour or reſpect, but that equal
Juſtice is due to the worſt ſo well as beſt men, and that he comes
firſt in order of time.

1. *John* in 1649. was by Order of the then Parliament tryed
for his Life, with an intent (I believe) of taking him away, but
the Jury not finding him Guilty, he was immediately, according
to Law, generouſly ſet at liberty by thoſe, that had quarrell e-
nough againſt him. This Example in the Parliament of keeping
to the Laws in the Caſe of one, who was a profeſſed implacable
Enemy to them, ought to have been Copied by *Cromwell*; but
in the contrary, to ſhew that there was a difference betwixt his
and his Predeceſſors (the Long Parliaments) Principles, when
the Law had again upon a ſecond Tryal (occaſioned by *Oliver*)
Cleared

Cleared *Lilburne*, the Parliaments submitting to the Law was no Example to him; For, contrary to Law, he kept him in Prison, untill he was so far spent in a Consumption, that he onely turned him out to dye.

2ly. Mr. *Conyes* Cafe is so notorious, that it needs little more than naming : He was a Prisoner at *Cromwells* Suit, and being brought to the Kings Bench Barr by a *Habeas Corpus*, had his Counsell taken from the Barr, and sent to the *Tower* for no other reason, than the pleading of their Clients Cause; an Act of Violence, that I believe the whole Story of *England* doth not parallel.

3ly. Sir *Henry Vaine*, above any one Person, was the Author of *Olivers* Advancement, and did so long, and cordially Espouse his Intereft, that he prejudiced himself (in the opinion of some) by it, yet so ungratefull was this Monster of Ingratitude, that he ftudied to deftroy him, both in Life and Eftate, becaufe he could not adhere to him in his Perjury and Falsenefs. The occafion he took was this, He appointing a Publick Day of Humiliation, and seeking of God for him, invited all Gods People in his Declaration, to offer him their advife in the weighty affairs then upon his fhoulders : Sir *Henry* taking a rife from hence offered his Advife by a Treatife, called *The Healing Question*; But *Cromwell*, angry at being taken at his word, Seized, Imprifoned, and indeavoured to proceed further againft him, for doing only, what he had invited him to do; and fome may think, that Sir *Henry* fuffered juftly, for having known him so long, and yet would truft to any thing he faid.

4ly. In *Richards* Affembly, certain Prifoners in the Tower, under the then Lieutenant, and fome fent thence to *Jerfey*, and other places beyond the Sea, complained of falfe Imprifonment. Their Goalor was fent for, and being required to fhew by what Authority he kept thofe perfons in hold, produceth a Paper all under *Olivers* own Hand, as followeth. *Sir, I pray you feife fuch and fuch Perfons, and all others, whom you fhall judge dangerous men, do it quickly, and you fhall have a Warrant after you have done.* The nature of this Warrant was by *Richards* Affembly debated, and having firft *Richards* own Counfells opinion in the Cafe, as

Serjeant

Serjeant *Maynard*, &c. they Voted the Commitment of the Complainants to be Illegall, Unjuſt, and Tyrannical; and that firſt, becauſe the Warrant by which they were Committed, was under the hand of the then (as they called him) Chief Magiſtrate, who by Law ought not to commit any by his own Warrant. Secondly, becauſe no Cauſe was ſhewn in the Warrant; And Thirdly, (in the Caſe of thoſe ſent out of the reach of a *Habeas Corpus*, which in Law is a Baniſhment) becauſe no Engliſh-man ought to be Baniſhed by any leſs Authority than an Act of Parliament. And therefore, for theſe reaſons, they Voted farther, that the Priſoners ſhould be ſet at Liberty without paying any Fees, or Charges, but the turning out, and puniſhing the Lieutenant by the Aſſembly (for obeying ſo unjuſt a Warrant) was prevented by their ſodain diſſolution.

5ly. The Tyrany in the decemating a party reſtored to common Priviledges with all others, and the publick Faith given for it, by a Law made to that end, by the then powers in being, is ſufficiently ſhewed in the mentioning of it, only there is this aggravating Circumſtance in it, That *Cromwell*, who was the principal Perſon in procuring that Law, when he thought it for his advantage not to keep it, was the only Man for breaking it; But to the honour of his firſt Aſſemblie, next following, it may be remembred, that they no ſooner came together, than like true Engliſh-men, who are alwayes jealous of the Rights and Priviledges of the people, damned the Act of Decemation as an unjuſt and wicked breach of Faith.

The third Aſſertion of *Cromwells* knowing no honeſty, where he thought his particular Intereſt was concerned, is made good : Firſt (though therein he miſtook his Intereſt) in his odious and unjuſt Warr with *Spain*, without the leaſt provocations, meerly out of an ambitious and covetous deſign of robbing that Prince of his Silver and Gold Mines, and becauſe he judged it for his Credit to diſguiſe his unlawfull deſires, he proceeded in it, by imploying his Creatures in the City, to draw the Marchants to complain of Injuries done them by *Spain*, and to Petition for Reparations ; but by a croſs Providence, his Project had a contrary Succeſs ; for inſtead of anſwering his ſeekings, the Marchants re·

remonftrated to him, the great prejudice that a Warr with *Spain* would be to *England*, and fhewed, that that King had been fo farr from Injuring us, that he had done more for Compliance and preventing a breach with *England*, than ever he had done in favour of any other Nation; But when *Oliver* faw his Method would not take, he called the Remonftrators Malignants, and begun the Warr of his own accord, in which, he was highly ingratefull in defigning the ruine of that Prince, who all along had been moft faithfull to his Party.

Secondly, His Falfenefs and Ingratitude, appeared fuperlatively in turning out his Mafters, who had not onely advanced him, but made themfelves the more odious by their partial affection towards him, and in his doing it, with the breach of a pofitive negative Oath, taken once a year, when made a Counfellor of State, befides the breach of all other Ingagements, Voluntary Imprecations, Proteftations, and Oaths, taken frequently upon all occafions in Difcourfe and Declarations; and yet further (when he had turned them out) and left them void of Protection, and expofed them to the Fury of the People, in purfuing them with falfe reproachfull Declarations, enough to have ftirred up the rude multitude to have deftroyed them, wherever they had met them.

Thirdly, His want of Honour, fo well as Honefty, appeareth yet further, in that having, by a long Series of a feemirg pious deportment, gained, by his diffimulation, good thoughts in his Mafters, the Long Parliament, and by his Spiritual gifts, winded himfelf into fo good an opinion with his Souldiers, (men generally of plain breeding, that knew little befides their Military Trade, and Religious Exercifes) that he could impofe, in matters of bufinefs, what Belief he pleafed upon them; he made ufe of the credit he had with each, to abufe both, by many vile practifes, for making himfelf popular, and the Parliament and Army odious to one another; and becaufe the Artifices he ufed are too many to innumerate, I fhall but inftance in fome few; As his flie complaining Infinuations againft the Army to the Parliament, and againft them to the Army: His being the chief Caufe of the Parliaments giving rewards to his Creatures, and then, whifper-

C   ing

ing Complaints amongst his Officers, of their ill Husbandry : His obstructing the House in their business, by long drawling Speeches, and other wayes, and then complaining of them to his Souldiers, that he could not get them to do any thing that was good: His giving fair words to every one, without keeping promise with any, except for his own advantage, and then excusing all with forgetfullness : And his deserting his Major Generalls, in their decimations, crying out most against them himself, when he only had set them at work, because questioned by his Assembly, is not to be forgotten, &c. I would not be understood, to remember any thing here, in Favour of the Long Parliament, for what might be Wicked in him, might be Just as to them; And though, if what he did, had been for the Restauration of his Majesty, he might have been excused, yet being for his own Single Advancement, it is unpardonable, and leaves him a Person to be truly admired for nothing but Apostasie & Ambition, and exceeding Tyberius in dissimulation. I am not ignorant, that some thinks it matter of praise in him, that he kept us in peace, four years, and nine months; but that hath little in it, his Majesty having done the like, almost double his time, since his Return, with one fifth part of that number of Souldiers which he Commanded; though he, hath also had the trouble of pressing, and sometimes forcing Uniformity in Religion, which he found under severall Forms; whereas Oliver, kept the Nation purposely divided in opinions, and himself of no declared Judgement, as the securest way of ingageing all severall perswasions equally to him; which Artifice, together, with his leaving the Church Lands alienated as he found them, were all the true Principles of Policie that I know of, which he kept unto. The Honesty of these Principles, I referr to the judgement of every mans Conscience; but if we may judge of things by experience and success, they seem to have been very happy in the world; For in comparing the Condition of the Protestant Countries at present, to what they were in times of Popery, we shall find them abundantly more considerable now, than formerly; for in taking a true Survey of the Reformed Dominions, we shall discover them to bear no proportion at all in largeness, to the Popish, and that there is nothing, that

keeps

keeps the Ballance betwixt the two parties, but the advantage that the firft hath, in being free from the Bondage of the Church of *Rome*, and the latters being under it; For as the Church of *Romes* mercies, are (by their Principles) Cruelties; fo had they power anfwerable to the naturall richnefs of the Soyl of their Countries, and extent of their Territories, they would long ere this have fwallowed up the Proteftant Churches, and made Bonefires of their Members; but as God, in his Mercy and Wifdome, hath by his Over Ruling Hand of Providence, preferved his Church; fo for the Romifh Churches inabilitie to effect that which they have will, and malice enough to carry them on to do, there are thefe natural reafons.

Firft, There being generally of the Popifh Countries, above one Moyetie belonging to Churchmen, Monks, Fryars, and Nunns, who like Droans, fpends the Fat of the Land, without contributing any thing to the good of mankind, renders them much the lefs confiderable.

Secondly, Marriage being forbidden to all thefe Sorts, and Orders, occafions great want of people every where, (they being uncapable of any Children but thofe of darknefs) except in *France*, which is an extraordinary Cafe, proceeding partly, by not being fo fubject to *Rome*, as other Countries of that belief are; but efpecially from the Multitude of Proteftants, that are among them.

Thirdly, The blind Devotion of thefe People, carrying them on to vaft expences, in the building, and richly adorning of many needlefs and fuperfluous Churches, Chapells, and Croffes,&c. with the making chargeable Prefents by the better, and Pilgrimages by the meaner fort, to their Idolls, keeps all degrees under.

Fourthly, The many Holydayes, upon which, the labouring man is forbidden to work, adds much to their poverty.

But Fifthly and Laftly, The vaft number of begging Fryars, who living Idly, and purely upon the fweat of other mens brows, without taking any labour themfelves, makes it impoffible, for the lower fort of people, who thinks they are bound in Confcience to relieve them, ever to get above a mean Conditi-

on;

on; Now whofoever fhall ferioufly weigh and ponder thefe Circumftances, under which the Popifh Countries lyes, and confider the Reformeds advantage in being free from them, muft confefs it the lefs wonder, that the Evangelical Princes, and States, with their fmall Dominions, compared to the others great, are able to bear up againft them; and now as the alienation of Church-lands, the turning out the Romifh Vermin, the Priefts, Monks, Fryars, and Nunns, (who devour all Countries wherever they come) and freedom from the Popifh Impofition upon Confcience, hath mightily increafed the greatnefs of the Proteftant Princes, and States, to what they antiently were, and the not doing the fame in the Popifh Countries, keeps thofe Princes under; fo, even amongft the Reformed, where the Church Lands are moft alienated, and Liberty of Confcience moft given, they profper moft, as in *Holland*, and fome parts in *Germany*, with other places. *Holland* could not have fo farr exceeded *Zealand* and *Friefland* in Trade and Wealth as it now doth, (the former having rather more Conveniency for Trade than they, and the latter equal with them,) were it not that their largenefs in the Principle of Confcience, gives them the advantage, As the others narrownefs in it, is their difadvantage. I have obferved, that when Proclamations (or *Placates* as they call them) have been Iffued out by *Friefland*, (as they fometimes are) againft Diffenters, the fubtle *Hollanders* have rejoyced at it, as knowing they fhould get the more People, and confequently Trade, and Wealth by it. That wife Prince, the Elector Palatine) who, by the General confent of all Perfwafions in *Germany*, is, for Wifedom, the Honor of their Nation, had never re-peopled his Country fo much as he hath already done, had he not been free as to Liberty of Confcience; I knew a Gentlemen, who having had the Honor to wait upon this Prince at *Manheime* (a City of his burnt totally down in time of Warre) was one time in his Train, as he walked out to take the Aire, when the Prince obferving fome Peafants of a ftrange Country come into the Town, he (as is ufual with him when he meets Strangers) called them to him, and upon examination, finding them to be Fanatick *Switzers*, fled from the Prefbyterian

byterian rigour, either of *Bearne* or *Zurick*; After he had incouragingly difmiffed them, expreffed to this *Englifh* Gentleman his admiration at the folly of the Principle of Impofition upon Confcience, in this age of fo much Light; which he further faid, was now fo great, that he believed the Bifhops of *England* would give over their plea of *Jure Divino*; and this Principle in a Prince, whofe Art in Government is fo eminent, is worth obferving: As this Elector findes the benefit of this Principle, (fo the Emperor, who is too much ledd by the Jefuites) findes (in his hereditary Lands which were layed wafte by the Warre) the want of it, whileft alfo feveral Soveraign Bifhops, and Abbots in *Germany*, findes a neceffity of giving Liberty of Confcience, in their feveral Countries, to all forts of *Lutherans*, if not to others; Nay fuch is the profitable Nature of this Liberty, that in *Italy*, where a Tolleration cannot be pretended unto, even in thofe places where Connivance is moft, they profper moft, as at *Venice*, *Genoua*, *Lucca*, and *Livorne*, which are all the places that can be faid to be well-peopled in *Italy*. And on the contrary, *Denmark*, where Church-lands are leaft alienated, of any of the Reformed Countries, and the City of *Lubeck*, where, of all the free *Lutheran* Imperial Cities of *Germany*, Liberty of Confcience is leaft given, they thrive leaft in both places; So that, as in all Countries abroad, amongft all Perfwafions, where Church Lands are moft alienated, and Liberty of Confcience moft given, they thrive moft; So the wifeft Princes, and States, gives moft Liberty, and Converts Church-lands moft to Publick good. And I think it will alfo hold, that as this famous Kingdome, in the times of Popery, was in no meafure fo formidable as now it is; So before the Reftauration of our Hierarchie to their Lands, their hoording up the money which before went in Trade, and their difcourageing and driving into corners the induftrious fort of people, by impofing upon their Confcience, it flourifhed more, was richer, and fuller of Trade, than now it is; And I dare undertake to be a Prophet in this, That if ever any Proteftant Countrey, fhould be fo farr forfaken of the Lord as to be fuffered to turn

unto

unto Popery, thefe Obfervations will be made good in their vifible loffe of the Splendor, Riches, Power, and Greatnefs, that they now know.

Had *Cromwell* been a Perfon of an open prophane Life, his Actions had been lefs fcandalous; but having been a Profeffor of Religion, they are not to be pleaded for, neither can it be confiftent with Religion to palliate them which have been of fo much offence, and (as may be feared) made fo many Atheifts in the World; And I cannot but ftand amazed, when I hear him extolled by fome, not ignorant of his Practifes, knowing in Religion, and (as I hope) fearing God.

Now I will fuppofe, I may be fufpected to have been injured, or difobliged by *oliver*; but I can with Truth affirm, I never received either Good or Evil from him in all my Life, more than in Common with the whole Kingdom (which I think may be allowed to render me the more a Competent Judge in his Cafe;) and that I am fo farr from being moved unto this, out of any quarrel to him, that, as I have here mentioned, fome few of many Injuftices, and State-errors, that he was guilty of in his fhort time, If I were confcious of any thing more, during his Protectorfhip, worthy applaufe, than I have here mentioned, I fhould not envy it him, but freely remember it; and if any think I have not faid enough on his behalf, and too much to his difadvantage, I have this for my Buckler, that I wifh I could have faid more for him, and had known lefs againft him; profeffing, that befides what I have here hinted, I am wholly ignorant of any one Action in all his Four Years and Nine Moneths time, done either wifely, Vertuoufly, or for the Intereft of this Kingdom, and therefore that I am none of his Admirers, I ought to be pardoned by my Readers.

Much more might be faid upon this Subject, but this may fuffice to fhew, that if *Mazerine* (at the hearing of *olivers* death) thought

thought he had then reafon for calling him a Fortunate Fool, if he were now living he would finde more Caufe for it, *Cromwell's* Lott, as to Reputation, having been exceedingly much greater fince his death, than whilft he was in the World : And that from forgetfulnefs of his impolitick Government, (from whofe Entrance we may date the commencement of our Trades decay;) And (through want of memory) in mens giving to him the Caufe of our former Wealth and Profperity, which truly belongeth to others. But what opinion foever *Mazerine* may have had of *Oliver*, he was without all peradventure a Perfon of more than ordinary Wit, and no otherwife a Fool than as he wanted Honefty, no Man being wife but an Honeft Man.

F I N I S.